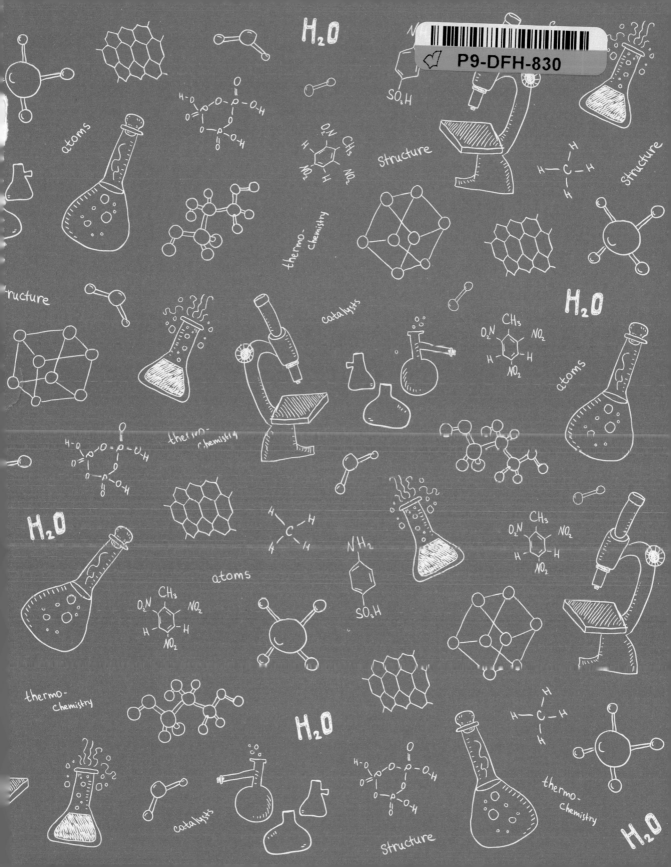

Kate the Chemist

THE BIG BOOK OF EXPERIMENTS

Kate THE CHEMIST

PHILOMEL BOOKS

THE BIG BOOK OF EXPERIMENTS

DR. KATE BIBERDORF

Philomel Books
An imprint of Penguin Random House LLC, New York

First published in the United States of America by Philomel,
an imprint of Penguin Random House LLC, 2020.

Philomel Books is a registered trademark of Penguin Random House LLC.

Visit us online at penguinrandomhouse.com

Library of Congress Cataloging-in-Publication Data is available.

Manufactured in China

ISBN 9780593116166

10 9 8 7 6 5 4 3 2 1

Edited by Jill Santopolo.
Design by Ellice M. Lee.
Text set in ITC Stone Serif.

It is important to keep safety in mind at all times. Children should ask permission from an adult and should be supervised by an adult whenever using sharp objects or kitchen appliances. The publisher and author are not liable for any injury that might result from the projects, activities, and experiments found in this book. Please see the below safety icons and make sure to observe them while experimenting.

SAFETY ICONS

CRYO-GLOVES / WORK GLOVES   LATEX GLOVES   GOGGLES   TRASH CAN   SINK   ADULT NEEDED

CONTENTS

INTRODUCTION

Hi! My name is Dr. Kate Biberdorf, but most people call me Kate the Chemist. You can usually find me teaching classes in Austin, Texas, or setting off explosions on national TV. For years, I've been bombarded with requests for at-home activities; so over summer break, I embarked on a mission to compile my *favorite* science experiments into one awesome book!

Do you know what chemistry is, besides being the best science in the entire world? It's the study of energy and matter, and their interactions with each other. Like how a gecko climbs a wall or how a rocket moves through space. If you follow the protocols (i.e., recipes) in this book closely, you will learn how both of these things happen. I'll even show you how to use unicorn glue and send a secret message to your BFF!

Every experiment can be done safely in your home with materials purchased online or in local pharmacies, craft stores, or home improvement stores. Just pay close attention to the safety icons and messiness levels to avoid hurting yourself (or your mom's favorite table).

Lastly, these experiments are better when shared with friends. So what are you waiting for? Call your bestie, grab your goggles—it's time for science!

XOXO,
Kate

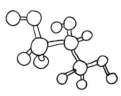

BUBBLE SNAKE

A Note From Kate: I did this experiment the first time I was on a TV show where I had to follow a script and couldn't just say whatever came into my head. I was so nervous about making mistakes, but I ended up having one of the best days of my life. On the very first take, the rubber band snapped and I accidentally poured colorful soap bubbles all over the main actor's head. Ah!!

Messiness Level: 3/3

Materials:

- 1 small plastic bottle
- 1 thin towel (or sock)
- 1 rubber band
- 3–4 drops food coloring (variety of colors)
- ½ cup water
- ¼ cup dish soap
- 1 small bowl
- 1 precision knife (or scissors)

PROTOCOL:

1. Have an adult use the precision knife or scissors to cut the bottom ½ inch off a plastic bottle. Go outside if you're worried about making a mess.

2. Use a rubber band to fasten the towel to the open side of the bottle.

3. Add the water and dish soap to the small bowl. Swirl to stir.

4. Add food coloring directly to the towel. Be creative—make a pattern!

5. Dip the towel into the soap solution.

6. Blow with force into the mouthpiece of the plastic bottle.

7. Check out your Bubble Snake!!

WHAT DO YOU THINK?

> Why did we add dish soap to the water solution?
> What is the gas trapped inside of the bubbles?
> What will happen if you double the amount of dish soap in the water solution?
> What will happen if you use a 2-liter soda bottle? Will the bubbles be bigger?
> What will happen if you use a thick towel instead of a thin towel?

HOW It WORKS:

When people breathe out, their breath contains primarily nitrogen, oxygen, and carbon dioxide. When we blow into the plastic bottle, all of these gases are trapped inside of the bubbles! This means that the bigger your exhale, the longer the bubble chain. The towel also plays an important role in this experiment. The dish soap is absorbed into the towel fibers until we use our breath to push our exhaled gas into a bubble. You may notice that some towels work better than others; the best ones are thick enough to absorb the bubble solution, but thin enough that you can easily push air through the fibers.

Why do we add the food coloring to the towel instead of the water solution? Ideally, we would like to create a multicolored chain of bubbles. If we add the food coloring to the towel, we can maintain sections of orange, red, green, blue, purple, etc. This is perfect for creating a rainbow bubble chain. However, if we add all of these colors to the water solution, our water will turn black. That solution would give us a chain of black bubbles instead of a colorful Bubble Snake!

UNICORN GLUE

A Note from Kate: This glue recipe inspired one of the major scenes in my novel *Dragons vs. Unicorns*. After you finish gluing all sorts of things together, check out the first book of the Kate the Chemist series to see how the main character uses this glue to save the day!!

Messiness Level: 3/3

Materials:

- 1½ cup water
- ½ cup cornstarch
- ¼ cup corn syrup
- 2 teaspoons white vinegar
- 2 teaspoons food coloring
- ½ teaspoon glitter
- 1 unicorn horn
- 1 medium bowl
- 1 medium saucepan
- Craft sticks
- Hot plate or stove top
- 1 spoon

TO Make Your UNiCORN HORN

1. Get a piece of paper.

2. Draw a large triangle with a rounded bottom on the paper.

3. Cut it out.

4. Roll the paper into a cone and tape or glue it together.

5. Decorate your unicorn horn.

PROTOCOL:

1. Add all ingredients (except the unicorn horn, bowl, craft sticks, and spoon!) to a medium saucepan.

2. Heat the mixture over medium-low heat for approximately 7 minutes, stirring continuously.

   NOTE: Depending on your heat settings, it may take up to 20 minutes. Be patient!

3. The mixture will thicken into a frosting-like substance. This is the glue.

4. Take the saucepan off the heat and allow the glue to cool for 5 minutes.

5. Transfer the glue to a medium bowl.

6. Use craft sticks to spread your glue!

HOW IT WORKS:

Glue is extra sticky because it has both adhesive and cohesive forces. When we combine these two properties, we are able to glue anything we want together. Let's think about an easy example, like gluing a poster of the periodic table to the wall. When a molecule (formed when two or more atoms join together) likes to make bonds with other molecules, we say it has strong adhesive forces. The best glues have extremely strong adhesive forces because they have to stick to both the poster and the wall.

The cohesive forces allow the glue to stick to itself—just like peanut butter stays together in a clump. When a molecule likes to make a bond with itself, it has strong cohesive forces. A perfect glue sample has great adhesive and cohesive forces so that the poster is stuck to the glue and the glue is stuck to the wall (adhesive-cohesive-adhesive).

It's important to give the glue time to dry before testing its strength. As the molecules from the atmosphere interact with the glue, the water evaporates from the glue mixture. This process forces the glue to harden, activating the "glue" properties we love. The resulting hard glue layer is extremely strong and very difficult to break. The strength of the glue is determined by what it's made of and what it can stick to.

EDIBLE SNOT

A NOte FROM Kate: There is nothing funnier than eating snot in front of someone. I hope you can use this experiment to thoroughly gross someone out!

Messiness Level: 3/3

Materials:

- 3½ cups water
- 1 teaspoon food-grade sodium alginate
- 1 tablespoon food-grade calcium chloride
- 1 small saucepan
- 1 spoon
- 1 medium bowl
- 1 squirt bottle
- 3–4 drops green food coloring
- Hot plate or stove top

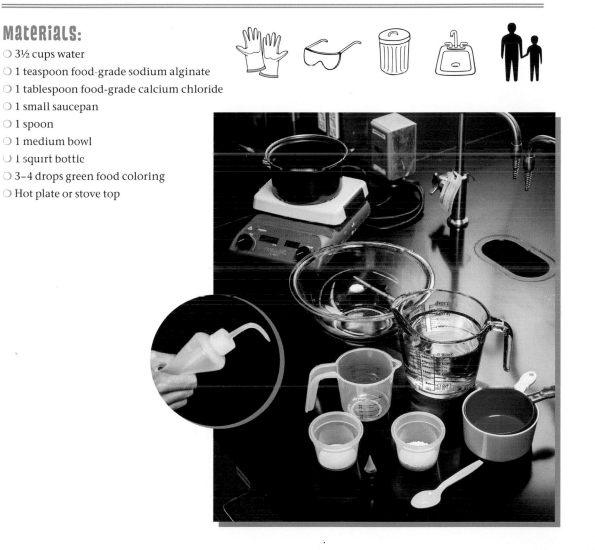

PROTOCOL:

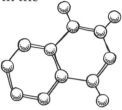

1. Add 1½ cups of water to the saucepan. (Reserve 2 cups for later in the experiment.)

2. Heat the water over low heat for 5 minutes.

3. Add sodium alginate to the water.

   NOTE: It will be clumpy and messy.

4. Stir continuously for 10 minutes. Use the spoon to break up clumps.

5. Remove solution from heat. Use the spoon to remove the remaining clumps from the solution.

6. Pour the smooth solution into the squirt bottle. You can use a pourable container to avoid spills.

7. Add green food coloring to the solution. Stir.

8. Add 2 cups of water to the medium bowl.

9. Add calcium chloride to the medium bowl. Stir until all of it dissolves.

10. Slowly squirt the green solution into the calcium chloride. If possible, try to squirt the entire solution in one continuous stream.

11. Wait 5 seconds!

12. Scoop the snot out of the bowl and enjoy your snack!!

> What happened when the sodium alginate was added to the water?
> Why did we need to heat the sodium alginate solution?
> What will happen if you use a bowl or spoon to add the sodium alginate to the calcium chloride?

HOW It WORKS:

This experiment is as fun as it is disgusting because we can actually watch an ion exchange happen in less than a few seconds! "Ion" is just a fancy word for an atom or molecule with a positive or negative charge. The sodium alginate and calcium chloride "exchange" cations (positively charged ions); during this process the alginate leaves the sodium ion to form a bond with the calcium ion. This is a favorable exchange (meaning the alginate is happier with calcium than with sodium) because the alginate and calcium ions can then alternate to form one extremely long snot polymer. A polymer is formed when lots of molecules join together, such as alginate-calcium-alginate-calcium. This happens because calcium carries a +2 charge, which means that it wants to connect to two alginate ions (one on each side)—just like you have two hands, so you can only hold hands with two other people at once.

The longer we allow our salt solutions to react in the medium bowl, the thicker our polymer casing will be. If I'm trying to really gross someone out, I let my snot sit for at least 3 minutes. Then I quickly bite into it to release the green snot liquid, getting the perfect reaction from my victim.

FAKE TATTOOS

A NOTE FROM Kate: When I went to Mexico, my friends and I decided to get beautiful henna tattoos as temporary souvenirs of the trip. I loved my seahorse so much that I wanted to try to re-create it when I got back home!

MESSINESS LEVEL: 2/3

MATERIALS:

- ○ 1 alcohol pad
- ○ 1 packet (or more) artificially flavored soft drink mix of desired color(s)
- ○ ¼ cup cornstarch per color (you can substitute baby powder if you have sensitive skin)
- ○ ¼ cup hot water per color
- ○ 1 cotton swab per color
- ○ Stencils (optional)
- ○ 1 paper towel
- ○ Liquid bandage
- ○ 1 small bowl per color
- ○ 1 spoon per color
- ○ 1 small saucepan
- ○ Hot plate or stove top

PROTOCOL:

1. Decide on the number of colors that you want to use in your tattoo.

2. Fill the saucepan with as much water as you will need, and heat over a hot plate or stove top at medium heat for approximately 5–7 minutes. Make sure the water is hot!

3. Add cornstarch and drink mix to a small bowl.

4. Repeat step 3 for each desired tattoo color.

5. Add ¼ cup hot water to each bowl and stir.

6. Use the alcohol pad to clean skin.

7. Dunk the cotton swab into the colored solution. Tap it on the side of the bowl to remove any excess liquid.

8. Draw the desired tattoo on the clean skin. Be creative or use a stencil!

9. Use the paper towel to lightly blot the tattoo, removing any extra liquid.

10. Wait 3–4 minutes for the liquid to evaporate. The tattoo will lighten. That's how you'll know you're ready for the next step.

    PRO TIP: For a multicolored tattoo, complete steps 7–10 for each color before adding the next color sequentially.

11. Apply liquid bandage over the entire tattoo.

12. Enjoy your new temporary tattoo!!

13. When you are ready to remove your tattoo, gently scrub it with soap and water (or a washcloth).

WHAT DO YOU THINK?

> Why do we wait for the water to evaporate from the tattoo before applying the liquid bandage?
> Why do we use the liquid bandage?
> What will happen if you use food coloring instead of the drink mix?
> What will happen if you combine different drink packets in one bowl?

HOW It WORKS:

Tattoos are a form of body painting that can be temporary or permanent. Permanent tattoos have been around for centuries, and have been used for a variety of purposes. Some tattoos have deep, symbolic meanings; others can be simply decorative. Since permanent tattoos require a big needle, I prefer to whip up my own temporary tattoo batter to test out different designs and decorations.

For our Fake Tattoos, we must wait for all of the water to evaporate after we finish drawing the cornstarch mixture on our skin. The process of vaporization is when a liquid turns into a gas. This physical change is endothermic, which means that it needs energy to complete the transition. You may be familiar with this process because the same thing occurs when a human sweats. We push sweat beads out of our pores, which then evaporate off our skin. The sweat takes heat from our body during evaporation, helping our body cool down during the process. For these tattoos, the water evaporates, leaving a colorful solid in its place. The tattoos are vulnerable to chipping, though, so we have to use the strong cohesive forces in a liquid bandage to keep them stuck to the skin.

SECRET MESSAGE

A Note From Kate: I would have traded my favorite goggles for this recipe when I was in middle school. We used to pass notes back and forth in class, and I would have loved to have sent a secret message!

Messiness Level: 2/3

Materials:

- ○ 1 piece of paper
- ○ 2 tablespoons table salt
- ○ 1 tablespoon hot water
- ○ 1 small bowl
- ○ 1 spoon
- ○ 1 paintbrush
- ○ Crayons (darker colors work best)
- ○ 1 small saucepan
- ○ Hot plate or stove top

PROTOCOL:

1. Pour water into the saucepan and heat on a hot plate or stove top.

2. Place the salt in the small bowl.

3. Have an adult help to add the hot water to the bowl.

4. Use the spoon to stir the salt solution for at least 1 minute to get as much of the salt into the solution as possible.

5. Dip the paintbrush in the salt solution and write your secret message on the paper. Try to use as much salt as possible.

6. Move the paper to a safe place and wait for it to dry completely. Be patient! This can take a few hours.

7. Carefully brush the extra salt off the paper.

8. Color over the entire paper with colorful crayons until the message is revealed!

WHAT DO YOU THINK?

> Why do we need to use so much salt?
> What will happen if you double the water?
> What will happen if you use a colored pencil instead of a crayon? Will the message still appear?
> What will happen if you use colored paper?

HOW It WORKS:

In order for us to write Secret Messages, we need to form a saturated salt solution. We do this by putting a lot of salt into hot water and forming the maximum number of interactions between the salt ions and the water molecules. We know our solution is saturated because we cannot dissolve any more salt in the water. Sometimes, we can even see the remaining salt at the bottom of the bowl! In these instances, we refer to the solution as a supersaturated solution.

The hardest part of this experiment is waiting for the paper to dry, but it is a crucial step in the protocol. All of the water must evaporate (a fancy word for when a molecule transitions from liquid to gas), leaving the previously dissolved salt crystals on the top of the paper. In this experiment, we remove all of the salt crystals that are visible to the human eye, but some salt actually remains in the paper fibers. These molecules are teeny tiny, but they are big enough to convey a secret message. When the crayon is rubbed over the paper, the salt crystals collect more crayon wax than the rest of the paper. The message is revealed as the salted sections darken to a much different shade!

ELEPHANT'S TOOTHPASTE

A Note from Kate: Elephant's Toothpaste is my most-requested experiment. When I perform this demonstration on television, I use 35% hydrogen peroxide, which can be quite difficult to find. This version uses materials that you (hopefully) already have in your household.

Messiness Level: 3/3

Materials:

- ¼ cup 3% hydrogen peroxide
- ¼ cup hot water
- ⅛ teaspoon active dry yeast
- ½ teaspoon dish soap
- 3–4 drops food coloring
- 1 8-ounce (236-milliliter) plastic bottle
- 1 medium bowl
- 1 pourable container
- 1 small saucepan
- 1 towel
- Hot plate or stove top

PROtOCOL:

1. Add water to the saucepan. Have an adult help you heat the water on medium heat for 3 minutes.

2. Add hot water to a pourable container.

3. Add yeast to the water.

4. Cover the container with a towel. Let it sit for 5 minutes.

5. Place the empty plastic bottle in the medium bowl.

6. Wearing gloves, add the hydrogen peroxide to the plastic bottle.

7. Add dish soap and food coloring to the hydrogen peroxide and gently swish to combine.

   PRO TIP: Drip different colors down the sides of the bottle to create striped toothpaste.

8. Quickly add the yeast mixture to the bottle.

9. Stand back and watch the Elephant's Toothpaste appear!!

   NOTE: Do not use this to brush your teeth!

WHAT DO YOU THINK?

> Why does the yeast have to sit in the water for 5 minutes?
> Why do we add dish soap to the bottle?
> What will happen if you use 6% hydrogen peroxide (available at most beauty stores)?
> What will happen if you use instant yeast?
> What will happen if you use a 1-liter bottle? How should you adjust the quantities of the starting materials?

HOW It WORKS:

This demonstration earned its name because of the foam that is released from the top of the bottle. In theory, the foam is so big that it could be used to clean an elephant's tooth. This is obviously a ridiculous notion, but how is the foam actually made? Well, we used yeast as a catalyst to trigger the beginning of the reaction. A catalyst is a special molecule that basically allows a reaction to take the highway instead of back roads to the final destination. Overall, the catalyst alters the pathway of the chemical reaction, giving us a faster way to form new molecules. In our experiment, the yeast is the catalyst, and it quickens the decomposition of the hydrogen peroxide.

Have you ever wondered why hydrogen peroxide is sold in a dark bottle? It decomposes (or the bonds within the molecule break) naturally when exposed to sunlight, which we can observe through the formation of small bubbles. Luckily, we are able to speed up this reaction by pouring the yeast into the hydrogen peroxide. As soon as the two substances mix, the yeast begins decomposing the hydrogen peroxide, releasing oxygen gas. The dish soap bubbles trap the escaping gas molecules as they push their way out of the plastic bottle. I like to host competitions to see who can have the bubbles come out of the top of the bottle for the longest amount of time. Are you up for the challenge?

SODA VOLCANO

A Note from Kate: I have one really bad habit. I drink diet soda. A lot. Too much, actually. But this means that I have plenty of diet soda at my disposal for science experiments. And this Soda Volcano is my favorite diet soda experiment.

Messiness Level: 3/3

Materials:

- ○ 1 full 3-liter plastic bottle of diet soda
- ○ 1 pack of porous candy with a sugar shell
- ○ 1 piece of computer paper
- ○ 2 toothpicks
- ○ Tape

PROTOCOL:

1. Fold the paper in half, hamburger style (the folded paper will be 8½ by 5½ inches).

2. Roll the paper into a tube with a 1¼-inch diameter.

3. Tape the paper together so it stays in its tube shape.

4. Poke a hole—just big enough for the toothpick to slide through—in the paper tube approximately ½ inch above the bottom [HOLE 1].

5. Poke another hole on the other side of the tube opposite the first hole [HOLE 3].

6. Poke another hole halfway between HOLE 1 and HOLE 3 [HOLE 2].

7. Poke another hole opposite HOLE 2 [HOLE 4].

8. Slide the first toothpick through HOLE 1 and HOLE 3.

9. Slide the second toothpick through HOLE 2 and HOLE 4.

10. Go outside.

11. Add 8–9 pieces of candy to the paper tube so that the candy is sitting on top of the toothpicks.

12. Remove the cap from the diet soda bottle.

13. Gently place the paper tube on top of the diet soda bottle. The tube should fit nicely inside the neck of the soda bottle, and the toothpicks should rest gently on the top of the bottle.

14. Quickly pull out one of the toothpicks to allow the candy to fall into the soda, pull the paper tube out of the soda bottle, and jump back!

15. Check out the Soda Volcano!!

HOW It WORKS:

Most sodas are composed of water, flavorings, and a sweetener. We used diet soda in this experiment because it contains artificial sweeteners that are not as sticky as sugar to clean up. Chemically speaking, though, both regular and diet sodas should work equally well for this experiment. Both sodas contain carbon dioxide, which is used to make the soda bubbly. The carbon dioxide gas is the catalyst for this experiment!

If you look closely at one piece of candy, you will be able to see tiny holes on its surface. These small holes are *perfect* for attracting small carbon dioxide bubbles. When one candy is added to the diet soda, the carbon dioxide gas swims to the candy to form bubbles on its surface. However, when 8 or 9 candies are added at the same time, all of the carbon dioxide gas is attracted to the candy at once. This causes the gaseous molecules to start slamming into each other and building up pressure. After a few seconds, there is too much pressure within the soda bottle, and the carbon dioxide shoots out of the top like a funky-looking volcano!

PUFFY SLIME

A NOTE FROM KATE: Puffy Slime is soooooo soft. I make this slime whenever I'm worried about something. The cloudlike texture is somehow very calming.

MESSINESS LEVEL: 3/3

MATERIALS:

- ○ 1 cup high-quality craft glue
- ○ 3 heaping cups shaving cream
- ○ 1 teaspoon baking soda
- ○ 2 tablespoons saline solution
- ○ 1 teaspoon (or more) food coloring
- ○ 1 teaspoon (or more) glitter
- ○ 1 medium bowl
- ○ 1 spatula

PROTOCOL:

1. Pour glue into a medium bowl.

2. Add 1 teaspoon (or more) of food coloring to the glue.

3. Add 1–3 teaspoons of glitter to the glue.

4. Stir the glue until it's all mixed together.

5. Add baking soda to the mixture in the medium bowl.

6. Add saline solution to the medium bowl.

7. Add shaving cream to the medium bowl.

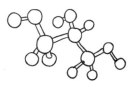

8. Stir the glue mixture for at least 60 seconds.

9. Allow the slime to sit for at least 3 minutes.

10. Play with the Puffy Slime!

PRO TIP: Add a few drops of saline solution to your hands to minimize the stickiness.

HOW IT WORKS:

Shaving cream contains a number of ingredients, but it is mostly water. When the button on the top of an aerosol can is pushed, air (which is gas) is squeezed into the liquid and a soft foam comes out of the can. A similar process happens when we blow bubbles in a glass of water. When the shaving cream is added to the glue, the trapped air bubbles give the slime its fluffy texture! The more shaving cream you add, the bigger and fluffier the slime will be.

We have to use saline solution for this experiment because we need boric acid and sodium borate to help us make a cross-linked polymer (a big molecule made of much smaller molecules). The boron reacts with the polyvinyl acetate in the glue mixture to make our slime flexible. How far can you stretch your polymer?

MAGNETIC SLIME

A Note From Kate: I can watch Magnetic Slime eat a magnet for hours. There is just something so spooky about slime that moves by itself.

Messiness Level: 3/3

Materials:

- ○ ½ cup high-quality craft glue
- ○ 4 tablespoons iron oxide powder
- ○ ¼ cup saline solution
- ○ 1 medium bowl
- ○ 1 plastic spatula
- ○ 1 neodymium bar magnet

PROTOCOL:

1. Pour glue into a medium bowl.

2. Have an adult help add the iron oxide powder to the glue.

    CAUTION: Do not breathe this in. Go outside to measure if you tend to spill things.

3. Stir the glue and powder until they're mixed together well.

4. Add saline solution to the mixture in the medium bowl.

5. Stir the glue mixture until all of the saline solution has been absorbed.

6. Allow the slime to sit for at least 3 minutes.

7. Wearing gloves, use your hands to knead the slime into a workable sphere.

    PRO TIP: Add a few drops of saline solution to your gloves to minimize the stickiness.

8. Use the neodymium magnet to play with the Magnetic Slime.

    CAUTION: Watch your fingers if you have two magnets. You can easily pinch your fingers between these super-strong magnets.

HOW IT WORKS:

When we add the iron oxide powder directly to the glue, we see the adhesion forces at work. These forces only happen when one molecule has a strong attraction to a different molecule. Stirring the two chemicals together allows for the iron oxide to wiggle itself into the pockets of the polyvinyl acetate (glue). Just as with our other glue experiments, the cross-linked polymer forms when the glue and borate (saline) ions alternate, this time creating a creepy black ball of slime.

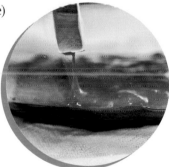

We added iron oxide to our slime because it is an extremely dense chemical that is magnetic at room temperature. This means that we can spike our slime with the black iron powder in order to give our gooey substance some magnetic properties. Copper and nickel are two other metals that do the same thing. In order to see the magnetic properties of iron, we have to use a neodymium magnet—traditional magnets are not strong enough to make the slime move!!

RAINCOAT

A Note from Kate: I love rockhopper penguins. They are the cutest, most adorable animals in the entire world, and I created this experiment to try to show how their feathers keep their bodies warm and dry!

Messiness Level: 2/3

Materials:

- ○ 1 piece of paper
- ○ 1 box of crayons
- ○ 1 squirt bottle
- ○ 1–2 cups water, to fill the squirt bottle
- ○ 2–3 drops blue food coloring
- ○ 1 baking sheet

PROTOCOL:

1. Using the crayons, draw your favorite feathered friend. My favorite is the rockhopper penguin!

2. Make sure every part of your animal has a layer of crayon, but leave the background completely empty.

3. Fill the squirt bottle with water.

4. Add 2–3 drops of blue food coloring to the water.

5. Cap the squirt bottle and gently swirl it to form a blue solution.

6. Place your drawing on a baking sheet.

7. Use the squirt bottle to cover the entire paper with water.

8. Look at the paper to see how the crayon feathers repel the water, and how they keep your feathered friend dry!

WHAT DO YOU THINK?

> What does the crayon wax represent in this experiment?
> How do feathers repel the water?
> What will happen if you use markers instead of crayons? Will the experiment still work?
> What will happen if you melt the crayons and use paintbrushes to apply the wax to the drawing?

HOW It WORKS:

Many feathered animals, like ducks and penguins, have a gland that forms a special oil that helps keep their bodies dry. The bird will find creative ways to roll around in this oil until all of its feathers are completely coated. The oil has a very important physical property: it is a nonpolar molecule. This means that all of the electrons (negatively charged particles) are evenly distributed across the molecule. A nonpolar molecule does not want to be anywhere near a polar molecule (such as water). In fact, the oil provides a protective layer over the feathers, repelling any rain or water that hits the bird.

We can use crayons to replicate the nonpolar/polar interactions between oil and water. Crayons are composed of wax, which is a nonpolar system with strong dispersion forces. When we covered our birds with the crayons, we added a protective layer of wax to the paper. The nonpolar properties of wax repel the polar properties of our blue water, just as feathers repel water or a raincoat shields us from rain. Have you ever noticed how water beads up on your raincoat? We tend to shake the water off our raincoats in the same way that birds shake the water off of their feathers. Neat, huh?

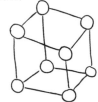

MOON ROCKS

A NOTE FROM KATE: I have always had a deep appreciation for space exploration. But until I can convince NASA to let me go to outer space, these Moon Rocks will have to keep me busy!

MESSINESS LEVEL: 3/3

MATERIALS:

- ○ 1 cup baking soda
- ○ 2 teaspoons water
- ○ 1 teaspoon food coloring
- ○ 1 tablespoon glitter
- ○ 1 lemon
- ○ 1 medium bowl
- ○ 1 pie plate
- ○ 1 knife

PROTOCOL:

1. Add the baking soda to a medium bowl.

2. Add 1 teaspoon of food coloring and 1 tablespoon of glitter (or more) to the medium bowl.

3. Wearing gloves, mix the food coloring and glitter into the baking soda until it's all mixed together.

4. Add the water to the baking soda mixture and stir until it starts to clump.

5. Wearing gloves, use your hands to shape the mixture into one large Moon Rock.

6. Place the Moon Rock on a pie plate.

7. Cut the lemon in half and quickly squeeze the lemon juice directly onto the Moon Rock.

8. Check out the alien activity!

WHAT DO YOU THINK?

> What happened when the lemon juice was added to the Moon Rock?
> What will happen if you sprinkle ½ teaspoon of baking soda over the Moon Rock before adding the lemon juice?
> What will happen if you slow the rate at which the lemon juice is added?
> What will happen if you stack multiple Moon Rocks into a snowman? Will they still react with the lemon?

HOW It WORKS:

Baking soda is a base (anything with a pH greater than 7) that contains sodium bicarbonate, and lemon juice is an acid (anything with a pH less than 7) that contains citric acid. When the lemon juice is added to the Moon Rock, a neutralization reaction occurs, which rapidly releases carbon dioxide gas (CO_2). The creepy alien activity is actually just the CO_2 gas escaping the Moon Rock! Luckily, the aliens do not seem to mind all the glitter.

My favorite way to vary this experiment is to create a deep crater in the Moon Rock. A crater is a round hole on the surface of the moon caused by a collision with a meteorite. This impact is so large that debris is often thrown everywhere. We can model this event when the lemon juice is added to the deep cavity: the gas builds up pressure, shooting debris straight out of the rock. Earth's moon has a lot of different craters, and they are named after a variety of people, including astronaut Buzz Aldrin!

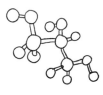

MAKE A PRESIDENT SCREAM

A NOTE FROM KATE: Have you ever wanted to talk to a former president? With this demonstration, you can finally interview the ghost of George Washington! 😄

MESSINESS LEVEL: 1/3

MATERIALS:

- 1 small piece of dry ice
- 1 small bowl
- 1 quarter

PROTOCOL:

1. Wearing a thick glove, place one piece of dry ice in a small bowl.

2. Push the quarter against the dry ice. Do not touch the dry ice with your bare hand.

3. Listen to President Washington scream!

WHAT DO YOU THINK?

> Why do we wear special gloves when handling dry ice?
> Will this experiment work with regular ice?
> Will the quarter ever stop screaming? Why or why not?
> What will happen if you use a nickel, dime, or penny instead of a quarter?

HOW IT WORKS:

Take a deep breath and exhale on the dry ice (solid carbon dioxide). What happened? Did you see the carbon dioxide (CO_2) turn into gas? At room temperature, dry ice will spontaneously change from the solid phase to the gas phase. During this process, billions of carbon dioxide molecules escape from the solid surface and move into the atmosphere. When we place the quarter on the dry ice, we trap all of these molecules that are trying to escape. The harder we push, the louder the noise. The CO_2 molecules are screaming "HELP ME! HELP ME!" as they try to escape from under the quarter. What happens when you use a penny or a nickel? How does the noise change? You should be able to prove to yourself that more molecules are trapped under the larger coins. Does this reaction work with any type of metal? Make a prediction and test it! Just be super careful not to burn yourself on the dry ice.

FOAMING SANDCASTLES

A NOTE FROM Kate: I came up with this experiment on a challenge to create "science" out of materials available at a beach house. I hope you enjoy my new twist on the classic sandcastle.

MESSINESS LEVEL: 3/3

MATERIALS:

- ○ 2 cups Play Sand
- ○ 5 tablespoons baking soda
- ○ 1 tablespoon plus 3–4 drops food coloring
- ○ 1 tablespoon dish soap
- ○ 1 tablespoon glitter
- ○ 1 lemon
- ○ 1 9-by-13-inch oven-safe dish
- ○ 1 medium bowl
- ○ 1 small bowl
- ○ 1 knife
- ○ 1 spoon
- ○ Oven

PROTOCOL:

1. Preheat the oven to 170 ° F.

2. Evenly distribute the Play Sand in a 9-by-13-inch baking dish.

3. Have an adult help to bake the sand for 30 minutes. Keep the oven door cracked to allow for circulation.

4. Use heat gloves to remove the sand from the oven, and stir the sand. If it is still wet, bake the sand for an additional 30 minutes.

5. Allow the sand to cool for 20 minutes, stirring every 5 minutes.

6. Add the dry, cool sand to the medium bowl.

7. Add 2 tablespoons of baking soda. (Reserve 3 tablespoons for later in the experiment.)

8. Wearing gloves, use your hands to mix the sand and baking soda together.

9. Add 1 tablespoon of food coloring to the sand.

10. Add dish soap to the sand.

11. Using gloves, mix the sand until completely combined.

12. Construct your favorite sandcastle on the 9-by-13-inch baking dish.

13. Add 3 tablespoons of baking soda to the small bowl.

14. Add 3–4 (or 20!) drops of blue food coloring and 1 tablespoon of glitter to the baking soda.

15. Use your hands to mix the food coloring and glitter into the baking soda.

16. Sprinkle the baking soda mixture around the sandcastle to create a moat.

17. Cut the lemon in half.

18. Squeeze the lemon juice over your creation to observe the Foaming Sandcastle!

CAUTION: Sand can ruin garbage disposals. Do your best to dispose of all sand in the trash can—not down the sink!

WHAT DO YOU THINK?

> Why did we bake the sand?
> How does the sand feel? Is it coarse?
> Does the sand maintain its shape? Why or why not?
> What will happen if you use flour instead of play sand?
> What will happen if you use orange or grapefruit juice on the sandcastles?

HOW It WORKS:

I found out the hard way that wet sand mixed with baking soda gives you a gross, clumpy mixture. I decided that I had to bake the sand for about 30 minutes in order to remove all of the water molecules from the sand. This seemed to work really well, but my best castles resulted from sand that was baked for 1 hour. I have such a hard time waiting to do science!

I love our sand because it has this fluffy texture that comes from the bubbles in the dish soap. If you want softer sand, you can add more dish soap. The soap is actually the most important part of this recipe because it is the reason our entire mixture sticks together. This happens whenever a molecule has both a hydrophobic and a hydrophilic side (like soap). Let's break these words down: *hydro* means "water," *phobic* means "afraid of," and *philic* means "fond of." So we have one side of the molecule that likes to bond to water and one side that does not want to be anywhere near water, giving us a fluffy, soft sand *perfect* for Foaming Sandcastles.

Lemon juice contains a molecule called citric acid. The citric acid reacts with the sodium bicarbonate in the baking soda in a neutralization chemical reaction. This process releases carbon dioxide gas, making our sandcastles foam and bubble! If you do not have a lemon, you can use a lime or orange (or vinegar) instead. Vinegar contains acetic acid, which neutralizes baking soda just like citric acid does.

GHOST

A Note From Kate: Halloween is my favorite holiday, which means that I love to come up with new demos that capture the spooky theme!! This ghost is so easy to make that I summon it all year round.

Messiness Level: 2/3

Materials:

○ 1 empty 3-liter soda bottle
○ 6 cups water
○ 3–4 drops food coloring
○ 10 pieces of dry ice (small enough to fit inside the soda bottle)
○ ¼ teaspoon dish soap

PROtOCOL:

1. Add water to the soda bottle.

2. Add 3–4 drops of food coloring and gently swirl the bottle.

3. Wearing thick gloves, add 10 pieces of dry ice to the soda bottle.

4. Observe the big ghost!!

5. If you want to try to catch the ghost, dip your fingers in water, and then put ¼ teaspoon of dish soap on your hands. Rub the soap across the rim of the soda bottle.

WHAT DO YOU THINK?

> What happened when the dry ice was added to the water?
> What color was the Ghost? Were you able to change the color of the Ghost?
> What will happen if you add dish soap to the soda bottle?
> What will happen if you use soda instead of water? Will the Ghost still appear?
> Touch the outside of the soda bottle. Is the bottle hot or cold? Why?

HOW It WORKS:

I tried this experiment using several different sizes of soda bottles, and I found that I liked the 3-liter bottle the best. With the larger soda bottle, I was able to add significantly more water to my experiment, which means that I could add a lot more dry ice! As soon as the dry ice hit the water, the carbon dioxide performed a physical change, rapidly releasing white gas. The more dry ice I added, the more molecules were able to convert into the gaseous phase. At a certain point, the molecules built up enough pressure to escape from the soda bottle, releasing the Ghost!!

We have to add enough dry ice to build up enough pressure to force the Ghost to actually leave the soda bottle. If you look closely, you can see that the gas starts at the bottom of the bottle and slowly moves up through the water. When it reaches the surface of the water, the gas quickly moves upward toward the soda bottle opening. As the number of molecules trying to leave the container increases, the number of collisions between the molecules increases. Think of it as a bunch of kindergartners trying to push their way through the doorway at recess—it's chaos! Every time the molecules bump into each other, they cause a collision that contributes to the speed at which the molecules leave the bottle. So if you want to make a big Ghost, you should encourage as many molecular collisions as possible!

POTATO NIGHT-LIGHT

A NOTE FROM Kate: It is rare that I find a science experiment that can be performed in the dark. I love that I can set this one up right before I go to sleep!

MESSINESS LEVEL: 1/3

MATERIALS:

- ○ 3 baking potatoes
- ○ 3 galvanized nails (or galvanized washers)
- ○ 3 pieces of copper wire (or 3 pennies)
- ○ 4 alligator clips
- ○ 1 LED light bulb (2.0–3.2 volts)
- ○ Pliers (if using wire instead of pennies)

PROTOCOL:

1. If you're not using pennies, use the pliers to cut 3 pieces of copper wire about 2 inches long.

2. Plunge 1 nail (or washer) into the left side of the first potato [NAIL 1].

3. Plunge 1 copper wire (or penny) into the right side of the first potato [COPPER 1].

4. Repeat steps 1–3 for the second and third potato.

5. Use one alligator clip to connect NAIL 1 and COPPER 2.

6. Use another alligator clip to connect NAIL 2 and COPPER 3.

7. Use another alligator clip to connect NAIL 3 and the negative side of the LED bulb.

8. Use the last alligator clip to connect COPPER 1 to the positive side of the LED bulb. If you do not know which side is positive/negative, guess! If it doesn't work the first time, flip the alligator clips attached to the bulb.

9. Enjoy your Potato Night-Light!

WHAT DO YOU THINK?

> What happened when all four alligator clips were finally connected?
> What will happen if you connect NAIL 3 to the positive side of the LED bulb?
> What will happen if you use a small digital clock instead of the LED bulb?
> What will happen if you use lemons or oranges instead of potatoes?
> What will happen if you use quarters instead of pennies?

HOW It WORKS:

Potatoes (and citrus fruits) contain an acid that allows for the transfer of electrons (negatively charged particles) between our two electrodes (a metal through which electricity can travel). In this experiment, the zinc in the nail/washer is the first electrode and the copper in the wire/penny is the second electrode. The electrons travel from the zinc through the potato to the copper electrode. From there, they move through the wire to the neighboring zinc electrode to repeat this process. The electrons eventually leave the last potato through the wire to power the light-emitting diode (LED). We just made a battery from potatoes!

NEON BRAINS

A Note From Kate: I have never once considered being a doctor or a surgeon because I cannot stand the sight of blood—it really creeps me out. I thought I could try to conquer my fear by creating a cute chemistry demonstration involving some human organs. I love this Neon Brains experiment, but guess what? Now I'm afraid of human organs too! Yuck!!

Messiness Level: 3/3

Materials:

- 1 cup
- 1 big piece of dry ice
  (about the size of an egg)
- 1 tablespoon dish soap
- 1 cup water
- 1 highlighter
- 1 black light
- 1 spoon
- Needle-nose pliers
- 1 baking sheet

PROTOCOL:

1. Place the cup on the baking sheet.

2. Add water to the cup.

3. Add dish soap and stir.

4. Use the pliers to remove the bottom plug from the highlighter.

5. Wearing regular gloves, remove the highlighter sponge from the highlighter casing, and squeeze the highlighter liquid into the water.

6. Stir the neon solution with the spoon.

7. Wearing thick gloves, add 1 piece of dry ice to the neon solution.

8. Shine the black light on the bubbles to see the glowing Neon Brains!!

WHAT DO YOU THINK?

> What is the white gas trapped inside the bubbles?
> Will the reaction still work without the dish soap?
> How will the reaction differ if you change the color of the highlighter?
> What will happen if you use tonic water instead of regular water?

HOW It WORKS:

When dry ice is added to water, the carbon dioxide quickly changes from a white solid to a white gas. This physical change is called sublimation, and it occurs when the distance between carbon dioxide molecules greatly increases. But in order for this endothermic transition to occur, the dry ice needs to take a lot of thermal energy from the water. You can prove this to yourself by touching the outside of the cup. The water has dropped in temperature, and the cup is very cold to the touch. The opposite of endothermic is exothermic, a process that releases heat during the reaction. Fire is a great example of an exothermic reaction, and it is way too hot to touch!

GLITTER BUBBLE VOLCANO

A NOTE FROM KATE: When I'm feeling a little creative, I pull out this experiment. You can build any structure out of the dough—one of my favorites is a burping penguin!

MESSINESS LEVEL: 3/3

MATERIALS:

○ 1 cup flour
○ ⅓ cup salt
○ ¾ cup baking soda
○ ½ cup water
○ 3–4 drops food coloring
○ 1 tablespoon glitter
○ ½ cup vinegar
○ 1 tablespoon dish soap
○ 1 large piece of dry ice
○ 1 medium bowl
○ 1 small bowl
○ 1 pourable cup
○ 1 spoon
○ 1 baking sheet

PROLOCOL:

1. Add flour, salt, and ½ cup of the baking soda to the medium bowl. (Reserve the rest of the baking soda for later in the experiment.)

2. Stir the solids together until they are thoroughly mixed.

3. Add ⅓ cup of water to the mixture and stir. (Reserve the rest of the water for the next step.)

4. Add 1 tablespoon of water and stir. Repeat until your mixture turns into dough.

   NOTE: All flours are different! Do not be afraid to keep adding water until you have a doughlike substance.

5. Shape the dough into a volcano on the baking sheet.

6. Wearing thick gloves, place the dry ice in the center of the volcano and cover it lightly with dough.

7. Remove the thick gloves, and gently smoosh the dough around the dry ice.

   CAUTION: Do not touch the dry ice when shaping the dough.

8. Add ¼ cup baking soda to the small bowl.

9. Add glitter and food coloring to the small bowl.

10. Use a spoon to stir the mixture.

11. Sprinkle the glitter mixture over the volcano.

    PRO TIP: For added effect, coat the whole outside of your volcano with the mixture.

12. Add vinegar and dish soap to a pourable cup. Use the spoon to stir.

13. Pour the vinegar mixture over the volcano and check out the Glitter Bubble Volcano!!

WHAT DO YOU THINK?

> What happened when the vinegar mixture was added to the volcano?
> What will happen if you use lemon instead of vinegar?
> Will the reaction still work without the glitter and food coloring?
> What will happen if no dish soap is added to the vinegar? Will the reaction still work?
> Why did we use flour to form the original volcano?

HOW IT WORKS:

I decided to use a simple dough recipe to construct the base of this volcano because I needed to have a sturdy structure that could withstand the production of lots of carbon dioxide gas. When the dough is first made, it should be mushy enough for us to create a volcano structure. The proteins in the flour make a strong volcano that will not collapse on itself when the reactions start to happen—just like the structure in a real volcano.

The Glitter Bubble Volcano is particularly unusual because it releases carbon dioxide as a result of two different chemical reactions. The first reaction that we see is the neutralization that happens when the acetic acid in vinegar reacts with the sodium bicarbonate in baking soda. Acetic acid is a weak acid (all acids have a pH less than 7), and sodium bicarbonate is a weak base (all bases have a pH larger than 7); this means that they will react together to form carbon dioxide and a salt. The bubbles that form on the surface of the volcano are bubbles from this neutralization reaction.

The big bubbles that erupt from the center of the volcano are produced by the reaction of the vinegar and the dry ice. The carbon dioxide in the dry ice takes the thermal energy from the vinegar and then changes from the solid phase to the gas phase. When a substance goes directly from a solid to a gas (without ever turning into a liquid), it is called sublimation. In other words, the carbon dioxide sublimed from dry ice into gas. While sublimation does not occur in real volcanoes, our system models the release of carbon dioxide during a volcano eruption very well.

DOUBLE BALLOON ROCKET

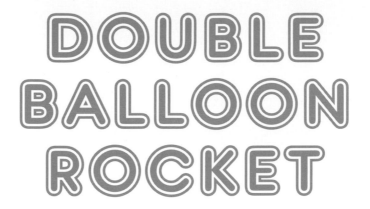

A Note from Kate: Warning: My 80-pound dog *hates* this demonstration. She chases my rocket across the living room and then barks at it incessantly. Wouldn't it be cool if we could explain science to dogs, too? I bet she would like my experiment then.

Messiness Level: 1/3

Materials:

- ○ 2 long balloons (like for balloon animals)
- ○ 2 wide straws
- ○ 2 light clamps (or binder clips)
- ○ Fishing line (30–40 feet)
- ○ Cardboard roll from a paper towel or toilet paper tube
- ○ Clear tape
- ○ Balloon pump
- ○ Scissors
- ○ A table

PROtOCOL:

1. Have an adult help you tie one side of the fishing line to a high corner of the room.

2. String the fishing line through the first straw [STRAW 1].

3. String the fishing line through the second straw [STRAW 2].

4. Tie the other end of the fishing line to an object in the lower corner on the opposite side of the room. Make sure the line is stretched tight!

5. Cut a 1-inch ring from the cardboard roll.

6. Inflate one balloon [BALLOON 1, green in this book], but do not tie it.

7. Thread the open end of BALLOON 1 through the cardboard ring, without letting the balloon deflate. The cardboard ring should fit around BALLOON 1 tightly.

8. Clamp the end of BALLOON 1 shut.

9. Place the balloon/ring apparatus on a table. Place the clamped side of BALLOON 1 on the right side of the table.

10. Inflate the second balloon [BALLOON 2, blue in this book], but do not tie it.

11. Starting from the left side of the cardboard ring, carefully thread the unclamped tip of BALLOON 2 through the ring without letting the balloon deflate. This will not be easy; take your time to push or pull the balloon tip until it appears on the right side of the cardboard ring.

12. Clamp BALLOON 2 shut.

13. Pull the cardboard ring down to the bottom six inches of BALLOON 1.

14. Point the clamped ends of the balloons toward the higher corner of the room. Carefully tape the cardboard ring to the lowest side of STRAW 1. Use another piece of tape to secure the highest side of STRAW 1 to BALLOON 1.

15. Use tape to secure the end of BALLOON 2 to STRAW 2.

16. Move the balloon rocket to the high corner of the room.

17. Quickly remove the clamp from the first balloon, then the second balloon, and watch the rocket propel across the room!

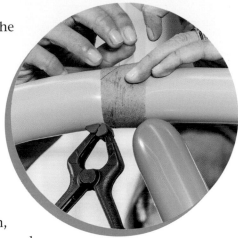

WHAT DO YOU THINK?

> What happened when the clamps were removed?
> Why did we string the fishing line from a high corner to a low corner of the room?
> What will happen if you switch the direction of the balloons?
> What will happen if you use only one balloon? Will the rocket still work?
> What will happen if you use ribbon instead of fishing line?

HOW IT WORKS:

Our Double Balloon Rocket acts just like rockets that go into space! The first balloon is the most important, because it is the one that is used to get the rocket moving. It releases air to push the rocket along the fishing line; the air molecules move out of the balloon in one direction, making the rocket move in the opposite direction. As soon as the first balloon has deflated, it detaches from the second balloon, triggering the second balloon to begin deflating. Our rocket finally stops moving once all of the air molecules have been released from the two balloons. What would happen if we added a third balloon to our model? Would the rocket be able to move faster? Farther?

DRY ICE BUBBLES

A Note FROM Kate: I will never forget the first time I helped someone catch a Dry Ice Bubble. Her jaw dropped, her eyes popped open, and she exclaimed, *"Whoaaaaaaa!"* She experienced science that day. Now it's your turn. 😊

Messiness Level: 2/3

Materials:

○ 4 cups water
○ 1 empty 2-liter soda bottle
○ ½ cup (or more) bubble bath solution
○ 1 dog bowl (or small bowl)
○ 1 funnel
○ 1 2-foot rubber tube
○ 15–20 pieces of dry ice (small enough to fit into the soda bottle)
○ Scissors (or precision knife)

PROTOCOL:

1. Put the end of the small funnel in one end of the tubing.

2. Cut a small hole in the top of the soda bottle cap.

3. Push the open end of the tubing through the hole in the top part of the cap. The cap should be about 3 inches up the tubing.

4. Add 4 cups of water to the soda bottle.

5. Add bubble bath solution to the dog bowl.

6. Wearing thick gloves, add 5–6 small pieces of dry ice to the soda bottle. Continue adding dry ice until a steady stream of white gas comes out of the top of the bottle.

7. Screw the funnel-tubing top onto the soda bottle.

8. Dip the funnel into the bubble bath solution.

9. Pull the funnel out of the solution and watch the dry ice bubble form.

10. Dip your hand into the bubble bath solution and try to catch the bubbles!

WHAT DO YOU THINK?

> What happened when the dry ice was added to the water?
> Why do we direct the gas through the tube? Would this experiment work with dry ice in the bubble bath solution?
> Why did we wet our hand before trying to catch the bubbles?
> What will happen if you start with ice-cold water? Will the reaction occur more quickly?

HOW IT WORKS:

Dry ice is a fancy type of ice because it is made of solid carbon dioxide (CO_2) instead of water. Most solid substances transition through the liquid phase before turning into the gas phase, but carbon dioxide is not like most substances. At room temperature, carbon dioxide transitions directly from a solid to a gas. This process is called *sublimation*, and it is an incredible physical change. What is important to note is that the bond between atoms does not break during this physical change. An atom is a unique collection of protons, neutrons, and electrons—the bond *between* the carbon atoms and oxygen atoms does not break during sublimation. Instead, the distance between carbon dioxide molecules gets bigger. Imagine that your stomach is the carbon atom and your hands are oxygen atoms, and that several human beings represent several carbon dioxide molecules. During sublimation, the distance between the humans gets bigger and bigger, but at no time does anyone's arm break in half. In other words, carbon and oxygen always stay connected, but the molecules get farther and farther away from each other.

There are many ways to form Dry Ice Bubbles, but in my opinion the funnel-tube-bottle apparatus is simply the best. When the dry ice is added to the water, it immediately grabs the water's thermal energy to release a large cloud of white gas. When enough pressure has built up, the gas is pushed through the tube and into the bubble bath solution. The bubble solution traps the white gas when creating a Dry Ice Bubble!

When your bubble finally pops, all of the gas dissipates, and you can no longer see the white color after a few seconds. Don't be fooled, though: the gas is still there! It's just so spread out that we can't see it anymore.

LEMON-LIME CLOCK

A NOTE FROM KATE: When we were kids, my sister and I started saying "Lemons" and "Limes" instead of "I love you." It's weird, I know. But if you're not weird, you're boring. This demo is for her.

MESSINESS LEVEL: 1/3

MATERIALS:

- 3 lemons
- 3 limes
- 6 galvanized nails
- 6 pieces of copper wire (or 6 pennies)
- 7 alligator clips
- 1 digital clock
- Pliers (if using wire instead of pennies)

PROTOCOL:

1. If you're using wire instead of pennies, use the pliers to cut 6 pieces of wire, each about 2 inches long.

2. Plunge 1 nail into the left side of the first lime [NAIL 1].

3. Plunge 1 copper wire (or penny) into the right side of the first lime [COPPER 1].

4. Plunge 1 nail into the left side of the first lemon [NAIL 2].

5. Plunge 1 copper wire (or penny) into the right side of the first lemon [COPPER 2].

6. Plunge 1 nail into the left side of the second lime [NAIL 3].

7. Plunge 1 copper wire (or penny) into the right side of the second lime [COPPER 3].

8. Plunge 1 nail into the left side of the second lemon [NAIL 4].

9. Plunge 1 copper wire (or penny) into the right side of the second lemon [COPPER 4].

10. Plunge 1 nail into the left side of the third lime [NAIL 5].

11. Plunge 1 copper wire (or penny) into the right side of the third lime [COPPER 5].

12. Plunge 1 nail into the left side of the third lemon [NAIL 6].

13. Plunge 1 copper wire (or penny) into the right side of the third lemon [COPPER 6].

14. Use one alligator clip to connect NAIL 1 and COPPER 2.

15. Use one alligator clip to connect NAIL 2 and COPPER 3.

16. Use one alligator clip to connect NAIL 3 and COPPER 4.

17. Use one alligator clip to connect NAIL 4 and COPPER 5.

18. Use one alligator clip to connect NAIL 5 and COPPER 6.

19. Remove the battery cover and the battery to expose the positive/negative side of the clock.

20. Use another alligator clip to connect NAIL 6 to the negative side of the clock.

21. Use the last alligator clip to connect COPPER 1 to the positive side of the clock.

22. Enjoy your Lemon-Lime Clock!

WHAT DO YOU THINK?

> What happened when we connected the lemon-lime circuit with the digital clock?
> What happens if you reduce the number of lemons and limes from 6 to 4 total? What happens if you use 10 total lemons and limes?
> What will happen if you connect NAIL 6 to the positive side of the clock?
> What other things can you power with your lemon-lime battery?

HOW IT WORKS:

Our lemons and limes form a battery that is strong enough to power a small digital clock. For it to work properly, the negative terminal on the clock must be connected to the nail, and the positive terminal must be connected to the copper wire. The electrons travel from the zinc through the lemon/lime to the copper electrode. From here, they move through the wire to the neighboring zinc electrode to repeat this process. The electrons eventually leave the last lemon/lime through the wire to the digital clock. What happens when you reverse the alligator clips? This action stops the natural flow of electrons from high energy to low energy. Batteries work as a result of the spontaneous travel of electrons from metal to metal; the electrons cannot flow in the opposite direction unless they have an external power source (like a battery). Can you imagine plugging your lemons and limes into the wall to recharge them?

DANCING RAISINS

A NOTE FROM KATE: I *love* to dance. I'm terrible at it, but I'm always the first person on the dance floor. Why let anything stop you from doing something that makes you happy? Making raisins dance makes me happy, too.

MESSINESS LEVEL: 1/3

MATERIALS:

- ○ 1 cup fresh tonic water
- ○ 5 small raisins
- ○ 1 tall glass

PROTOCOL:

1. Add 1 cup of tonic water to the glass.

2. Add 1 raisin to the tonic water.

3. Slowly add the second raisin to the tonic water.

4. Add the last 3 raisins slowly, 1 by 1.

5. Observe the raisin dance party!

WHAT DO YOU THINK?

> What happened when the raisins were added to the tonic water?
> What will happen if the tonic water is not fresh (i.e. if it's flat)?
> What will happen if you use tap water instead of tonic water?
> What will happen if you use seltzer water instead of tonic water?
> What will happen if you use dried cranberries instead of raisins?
> What will happen if you use grapes instead of raisins?

HOW It WORKS:

The tonic water is a carbonated beverage filled with carbon dioxide (CO_2) gas. Before the raisins are added to the glass, you can see small bubbles of CO_2 rising to the surface of the liquid. If you put your ear near the top of the glass, you can actually hear the bubbles popping! Gas solubility (a fancy word to describe how well the gas dissolves in the liquid) increases as the temperature of the liquid decreases, and vice versa. So if we heat up the tonic water, the CO_2 gas bubbles will move faster. I like to zap my tonic water in the microwave for a few seconds to increase the rate of bubble evolution.

When each raisin is added to the tonic water, some bubbles become trapped in the wrinkles of the raisin. After a few seconds, several bubbles are hooked on to the raisin, and it is carried to the surface of the water. The bubbles pop at the top of the glass, allowing the raisin to return to the dance party at the bottom of the glass. This process will continue until all the CO_2 gas has stopped bubbling. If you go outside, you can shake up the soda bottle, then add the raisins directly to the bottle to see a crazy dance party! What happens if we add the raisins to tap water? Unfortunately, tap water is boring and does not have any carbonation; all of the raisins sink to the bottom of the glass.

LAVA LAMP

A NOTE FROM KATE: My brother had a Lava Lamp in his room when we were growing up. He's 9 years older than me, so I have always associated Lava Lamps with "being cool." Now that I'm old enough to have my own Lava Lamp, I just had to make one that could be started on demand. Take that, Brendan!

MESSINESS LEVEL: 2/3

MATERIALS:

- ○ 2 cups baby oil
- ○ 2 cups water
- ○ 1 teaspoon food coloring
- ○ 1 effervescent tablet (or an antacid that contains sodium bicarbonate)
- ○ 1 empty 1-liter soda bottle

PROTOCOL:

1. Add all the water to the soda bottle.

2. Add 1 teaspoon (or more) of food coloring to the soda bottle.

3. Add all the baby oil to the soda bottle.

4. Crush 1 effervescent tablet into many small pieces.

5. Add the crushed tablet to the soda bottle.

6. Cap the bottle and watch the Lava Lamp eruption!

    PRO TIP: If you want your lamp to erupt again, add another crushed tablet (and another and another and another . . .).

WHAT DO YOU THINK?

> Did the oil and water mix? Why or why not?
> What happened when the food coloring was added to the solution? Did the food coloring move from the water to the oil? Why or why not?
> Why did we have to add the effervescent tablet to the Lava Lamp?
> What will happen if you use vegetable oil instead of baby oil?
> What will happen if you use a mason jar instead of a soda bottle? What about a cup?

HOW It WORKS:

Water and oil are both liquids, but they have different densities. The word density describes the amount of material in a specific volume (or the 3-D space occupied by the material). Water has the perfect density because 1 gram occupies exactly 1 milliliter. In our demonstration, the water is heavier than the oil, so it sinks to the bottom of the soda bottle. This means that the oil is lighter and less dense than water.

Water and oil molecules have different shapes. Oil is long and thin like spaghetti, and water is pointy like a triangle. For water, the oxygen atom is one point of the triangle, and the hydrogen atoms are at the other two corners. What's particularly neat about water is that the oxygen atom attracts the electrons from the hydrogen atoms, making water a polar molecule. In contrast, oil does not have any special atoms that can collect electrons; therefore, oil is a nonpolar molecule. Polar and nonpolar molecules do not mix well, which is another reason why oil and water form two separate layers.

The effervescent tablet reacts with water to release carbon dioxide gas. When the gas bubbles rise to the surface of the liquid, they pull water droplets with them through the oil layer. The gas bubbles pop when they reach the surface, allowing for the water to drop back down to the bottom of the soda bottle. The process repeats until the effervescent tablet stops producing carbon dioxide gas. Do not worry, though—you can just add another tablet to restart the reaction!

TRAPPED TORNADO

A NOTE FROM KATE: There was a short period of time in my life when I wanted to be a storm chaser. I'm a bit of an adrenaline junkie, and I idolized the scientists on TV who chased storms. I love the idea of feeling the winds of a tornado whipping around me. Well, my mom never let me do that, so I decided to trap a tornado in a bottle instead.

MESSINESS LEVEL: 3/3

MATERIALS:

- ○ 2 empty 1-liter soda bottles
- ○ 1½-inch metal washer
- ○ 1 liter water
- ○ 2–3 drops food coloring
- ○ ¼ teaspoon glitter
- ○ Heavy-duty tape

PROTOCOL:

1. Fill 1 soda bottle with water.

2. Add food coloring and glitter to the water.

3. Place the metal washer over the top of the soda bottle.

4. Turn the second soda bottle upside down, and place it on top of the washer on the first soda bottle.

5. Use *lots* of heavy-duty tape to secure the second soda bottle.

6. Turn the whole apparatus upside down. Swirl.

7. Check out the tornado!

WHAT DO YOU THINK?

> What happened to the glitter? Did it stay in one soda bottle?
> What will happen if you add oil to the mixture before making the tornado apparatus?
> What will happen if you add one squirt of dish soap to the water?
> What will happen if you use two 2-liter soda bottles? Will the experiment work as well?
> How long does it take for all of the water to drain into the bottom soda bottle? Is there a way to increase (or decrease) this rate?

HOW IT WORKS:

The construction of the Trapped Tornado apparatus is very important. We need an extremely tight seal in order for our tornado to work properly. To be honest, I love anything that will give me a reason to use an excessive amount of tape, especially in the name of science!

If the bottles are sealed together perfectly, the air and water will not be able to move from one bottle to the other on their own, regardless of which substance is in the top bottle. This phenomenon seems to defy gravity when the water bottle is on top, but we have to remember that billions of gaseous molecules are taking up all the space in the bottom bottle.

But if we can find a way to form a vortex, we can transfer the air from the bottom bottle to the top bottle, allowing the water to fall to the bottom

bottle. The vortex is formed when the water spins around the top bottle, creating a small opening in the center of the tornado. When this happens, the air immediately rushes through the center of the vortex, essentially powering the tornado. Now we have an unstoppable force that will continue to spin until all of the air has rushed up through the small opening and filled the top bottle. Real tornadoes are also powered by central air currents, which is why tornadoes often start in big, open (windy) fields.

SNOW

A NOTE FROM KATE: I grew up in Michigan, which means my favorite memories include snow, hot chocolate, and warm fuzzy blankets. This is my gift to those of you who have never had that experience.

MESSINESS LEVEL: 2/3

MATERIALS:

- ○ 1 teaspoon sodium polyacrylate (you can find this inside disposable diapers if you cut them open)
- ○ 4 teaspoons water
- ○ 3–4 drops food coloring
- ○ 2 small cups

PROTOCOL:

1. Place sodium polyacrylate in one cup.

2. Add the water to the empty cup.

3. Add 3–4 drops (or more) of your favorite food coloring to the water.

4. Quickly pour the colored water into the cup with sodium polyacrylate.

5. Check out the snow!

WHAT DO YOU THINK?

> What does the snow feel like? Is it hard or soft? Squishy or prickly?
> Is there any water left in the cup? If not, where did it go?
> Can you make a snowball with your new snow? Why or why not?
> What will happen if you add the sodium polyacrylate to the water instead of the water to the polymer?
> What will happen if you use milk instead of water?

HOW IT WORKS:

Sodium polyacrylate is a polymer that absorbs water! This polymer is called a superabsorbent polymer because it can absorb up to 200 times its mass in water. I like to think of the polymer as a bug wearing a big jacket with lots of pockets. This bug grabs each water molecule and puts it into the pockets of the jacket. The jacket gets bigger and bigger until the bug has placed all of the water in the jacket pockets (just like the snow absorbed all of the water).

What's neat about this polymer is that it can actually desorb all of the water that it originally absorbed. If you put your snow outside for a week (especially in Texas, where I live now), all of the water will evaporate, and you will be left with the original powder. You can do this experiment over and over again, but your snow will be permanently dyed by the food coloring.

HOT ICE

A NOTE FROM KATE: I grew up playing in the freezing cold weather in Michigan. At the end of a long outdoor play session, we would shiver in the mudroom and daydream about a form of snow/ice that would not make our fingers and toes go numb. After years of searching, I think I may have finally found it!

MESSINESS LEVEL: 2/3

MATERIALS:

- ○ 1 cup sodium acetate trihydrate
- ○ 2 tablespoons distilled water
- ○ 2–3 cups regular water
- ○ 1 medium saucepan
- ○ 1 Pyrex glass (heat-safe)
- ○ Hot plate or stove top
- ○ Towel or trivet
- ○ 1 spoon

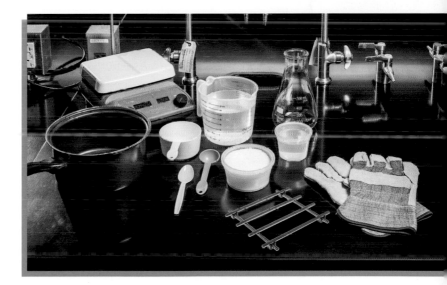

PROTOCOL:

1. Add the sodium acetate and the distilled water to the Pyrex glass. Save at least 1 crystal of sodium acetate for later.

2. Fill the saucepan halfway with water.

3. Place the glass directly in the saucepan.

4. Heat the water/glass on low heat until all of the sodium acetate has dissolved (about 15 minutes). Stir the solution every few minutes.

5. Wearing heat gloves, carefully remove the glass from the saucepan.

6. Set the glass aside on a towel or a trivet until it has completely cooled (a few hours).

   CAUTION: This experiment is very sensitive. Make sure you don't accidentally bump into the flask and start the reaction!

7. Add *one* crystal of sodium acetate to the glass and watch the ice instantly appear!!

   ALTERNATIVE: Put one crystal on a flat surface, pour the solution over it, and grow a stalagmite!

WHAT DO YOU THINK?

› Why did we have to heat the salt solution?
› Why did we have to wait for all of the sodium acetate to dissolve?
› Why did we use distilled water instead of tap water in this experiment?
› What happened when the crystal was added to the solution?

HOW It WORKS:

Sodium acetate is a really neat ionic compound. The white solid does not dissolve easily in water, but we can make it happen by heating it up when it's mixed with water. After only a few minutes, it all dissolves to form a yellow-tinted solution. On a microscopic level, here's what happens: the positive sodium ions are surrounded by the partially negative oxygen atoms from water; meanwhile, the negative acetate ions are surrounded by the partially positive hydrogen atoms from water. These interactions are very strong, which is why the solution can then cool to room temperature without reforming the white solid.

But even though these bonds are freaky strong, they are extremely fragile. We were able to see this when one crystal triggered the Hot Ice chain reaction. The positive and negative charges carried by the sodium acetate crystal mess up the newly formed bonds, forcing the entire solution to spontaneously form a hot solid. Can you feel the heat through the glass? This reaction is exothermic, which means it releases heat as the products are formed. Have you ever used hand warmers to withstand the cold weather for long periods of time? They use the same sodium acetate reaction to keep your fingers and toes warm!

PRO TIP: Your hand warmers can be recharged by dunking them in hot water for 15 minutes and then allowing them to cool completely—just like we did when we prepared the Hot Ice solution!

This book is dedicated to every father who
encouraged their daughter to play in the mud.

Dad, every little girl deserves a father like you.

—*K. B.*

ACKNOWLEDGMENTS

This book would not have been possible without the support and encouragement of the entire Kate the Chemist Team: my editor Jill Santopolo, assistant editor Cheryl Eissing, publisher Ken Wright, art director Ellice Lee, designer Lori Thorn, photographer Dustin Meyer, my assistant Jacks Reyna, my first chemistry teacher Kelli Palsrok—and the dynamic duo: manager Glenn Schwartz and agent Albert Lee.

I owe much to my parents for letting me turn their bathroom into my first lab, and to my husband Josh for pushing me to make bigger and better experiments. I would like to thank everyone at Penguin Young Readers and Philomel Books for helping me turn my dream into a reality.